CW01082834

Original title:
A Life of Passion

Editor: Theodor Taimla
Author: Isabella Ilves
ISBN HARDBACK: 978-9916-763-94-0
ISBN PAPERBACK: 978-9916-763-95-7

Invincible Heartbeats

In the depths where shadows creep,
Resilience stirs, awake from sleep.
With every challenge we embrace,
Our spirits rise, finding grace.

Through battles fought and scars we bear,
A pulse of courage fills the air.
Fear may whisper, doubts may shout,
But this heart will not give out.

Echoes of strength in every breath,
Life's rhythm dances, conquering death.
Against the tide, we stand our ground,
In our hearts, the power is found.

With every heartbeat, dreams ignite,
An undying flame, burning bright.
Together we rise, never apart,
Fueled by the fire of each strong heart.

In the quiet, let courage sing,
An invincible force, a sacred thing.
With hope entwined in every beat,
We are unstoppable, we are complete.

Chasing Celestial Trails

Under the starlit skies, we roam,
Whispers of the night guide us home.
Every twinkle sings a song,
In the universe, we belong.

With each comet's blaze, we chase,
Dreams are woven through time and space.
Moonlight dances on our skin,
A cosmic journey to begin.

Constellations map our way,
Through the darkness, we shall sway.
Galaxies spin in our eyes,
As we travel to distant skies.

Wish upon a falling star,
In this vastness, we are never far.
With every pulse, we feel the thrill,
A chase that time can never still.

In the silence of the night,
Our hopes take flight, shining bright.
Chasing trails of dreams anew,
Through celestial paths, we pursue.

Kaleidoscope of Yearning

Colors dance in endless night,
Whispers of dreams take their flight.
A heart that longs, a soul that seeks,
In every hue, a love that speaks.

Fractured moments blend and sway,
Fragments of hope in twilight's play.
Every shift, a new desire,
A canvas filled with longing fire.

The Path of Boldness

Steps unfurl on daring ground,
With every heartbeat, courage found.
Facing fears, the shadows flee,
A journey forged, the wild and free.

Voices rise, a steady song,
Together where brave hearts belong.
Through storms and trials, we advance,
On paths of boldness, a fearless dance.

Vibrations of a Courageous Spirit

Feel the pulse of the earth beneath,
A symphony of strength we breathe.
In the waves of fear, we stand tall,
With every tremor, answering the call.

A whisper travels on the breeze,
Courage ignites with gentle ease.
Through valleys deep and mountains high,
Our spirits soar, learning to fly.

Each heartbeat echoes resilience rare,
In the face of storms, we declare.
Brave hearts laughing in the dark,
Together we rise, igniting the spark.

With every step, we shatter doubt,
A melody of hope, singing out.
Vibrations guide us, free and wild,
In the dance of life, we are beguiled.

Embrace the strength that lies within,
A courageous spirit, ready to begin.
In every moment, we find our way,
Vibrations of courage lead the day.

The Spirit's Ascent

Mountains call with ancient grace,
Guiding spirits to embrace.
Through the clouds and into blue,
The heart ignites, the soul breaks through.

Winds of change sweep through the air,
Lifting burdens, light as prayer.
Within the silence, truth will rise,
A journey met with endless skies.

Across the Canopy of Stars

Beneath the sky so wide and deep,
Dreams and wishes gently creep.
Whispers float on lovers' sighs,
Carried forth where silence lies.

Constellations tell their tales,
Of ancient ships and wind-filled sails.
Guided by the moon's soft glow,
Through the night, our spirits flow.

Stars like diamonds, bright and pure,
In their light, we find a cure.
Hope ignites with every spark,
Filling souls that wander dark.

Each twinkle holds a secret fate,
A promise made, a dance innate.
In this vastness, hearts align,
Across the heavens, yours and mine.

Together we will forge ahead,
With stardust dreams, our future's thread.
Life unfolds in cosmic beams,
Across the canopy of dreams.

Emotions Under the Stars

Stars above, a silent watch,
Hearts entwined, no need to hutch.
Underneath the cosmic light,
Feelings bloom in the deep night.

Whispers shared like secret spells,
Echoes of love where silence dwells.
In constellations, dreams take flight,
Guided by the moon's soft light.

Portraits of Uncharted Seas

Gaze upon the ocean's face,
Waves unravel in a wild embrace.
Each crest a story waiting to unfold,
Portraits painted in shades of gold.

Beneath the surface, secrets reside,
Mysteries linger with the tide.
In the depths, dreams softly gleam,
Reflections of every sailor's dream.

With every gust, the sails unfurl,
Adventures beckon in this vast whirl.
The horizon calls, an open door,
To chart new courses, to explore.

Within the storms, we find our voice,
Courage born from every choice.
The waves may crash, the tempest roar,
But we are sailors, seeking more.

On uncharted seas, we make our mark,
Navigating through the light and dark.
In every tempest, we will rise,
Crafting portraits beneath open skies.

The Journey's Anthem

With every step, a story spun,
A path that glows beneath the sun.
We tread on roads both new and old,
In every heart, a dream unfolds.

Mountains rise, like dreams that soar,
Valleys whisper, calling more.
Each turn reveals a fleeting glance,
Of life's grand, intricate dance.

The winds of change begin to sing,
A symphony of hope, they bring.
Every challenge, a call to strive,
With every heartbeat, we survive.

As rivers carve the land so true,
We navigate with hearts anew.
The journey's song will guide our way,
To brighter dawns and hopeful days.

In every triumph, tears may fall,
Yet love's embrace will conquer all.
With every mile, our spirits grow,
In the journey's anthem, we will glow.

Embracing the Eternal Flicker

In shadows cast by time's soft hand,
We find a light, like grains of sand.
An ember glows within the night,
A beacon warm, a guide so bright.

Through valleys deep and mountains high,
Love's flicker dances in the sky.
In quiet moments, it remains,
A flame that soothes all life's pains.

Glimmers spark in tender hearts,
In every end, a new start parts.
With every flicker, life ignites,
Embracing dreams on starry nights.

In laughter shared and tears that flow,
The flicker's warmth begins to grow.
Together in this fragile space,
We find our strength, our sacred grace.

So let us hold this light so near,
Through trials faced, we'll persevere.
Within our souls, that flicker thrives,
Embracing love, it keeps us alive.

Dance of Unwavering Resolve

Beneath the storm, we plant our feet,
With hearts united, strong and sweet.
Each drop of rain, a test we face,
In every struggle, we find grace.

The winds may howl, the night may fall,
Yet we stand tall, we hear the call.
With courage forged in fire's glow,
We'll dance along, our spirits flow.

Through shadows thick and doubts that creep,
Our bond will hold, our dreams will leap.
Each step a mark, a rhythmic beat,
In this grand dance, we won't retreat.

Together we embrace the fight,
With every challenge, we'll take flight.
The world may shake, but we will rise,
With unwavering resolve, we touch the skies.

In unity, we brave the night,
With hearts ablaze, we'll find the light.
Through life's vast stage, we will advance,
Together in this daring dance.

Journey Through the Stars

In velvet skies, the stars do gleam,
A dance of light, a fleeting dream.
Galaxies whisper, secrets unfold,
Each twinkle tells a tale of old.

Through cosmic seas, our spirits sail,
On stardust wings, we shall prevail.
With every world that we explore,
The universe opens every door.

Nebulae cradle, radiant glow,
Guiding our hearts where few can go.
A symphony of silence rings,
As we embrace what starlight brings.

Winds of time brush past our face,
In the embrace of endless space.
Weaving dreams in astral seams,
Awake or lost, we chase our dreams.

With every breath, a wish is cast,
Leaving behind both present and past.
Boundless night, forever bright,
In our hearts, we chase the light.

Songs of the Wanderlust

Wanderlust sings in gentle tones,
A call to those who roam alone.
Footsteps tracing paths unknown,
In search of sights, we make our own.

Mountains rise, a challenge bold,
Stories whispered, adventures told.
Across the valleys, rivers flow,
Each journey brings a chance to grow.

Beneath the skies, both storm and sun,
We find the peace where we begun.
Roads untraveled lead us far,
In every heart, we hold a star.

With open arms, we dance with fate,
Embracing all, we celebrate.
The world unfolds in vibrant hues,
A canvas bright, awaiting views.

In every place, a tale to weave,
In every moment, we believe.
Songs of wander fill the air,
A melody that leads us there.

Alchemy of Dreams

In twilight's hush, the dreams take flight,
Crafted whispers in the night.
Golden visions blend and swirl,
A tapestry of thoughts unfurl.

Magic brews in the mind's embrace,
Transforming shadows into grace.
Each dream a seed in silence sown,
From hidden depths, new worlds are grown.

Through silver gates, we drift and sway,
In realms where night replaces day.
A dance of thoughts, a gentle stream,
We dive into the fabric of dream.

With every hour lost in trance,
We rearrange the cosmic dance.
Alchemy spins, a potion bright,
Brewing wonders veiled in light.

Awakened souls, we chase the flare,
In the alchemy, we dare to share.
Through shared dreams, we find our themes,
Uncovering life's forgotten schemes.

Embrace of the Infinite

In the stillness, whispers swell,
An echo from the cosmic well.
Boundless love, a gentle tide,
In the embrace where dreams abide.

Time dissolves in sacred breath,
Infinity spins, teasing death.
Moments merge, the past and now,
In unity, we take a bow.

Hearts aligned like stars above,
In this space, we learn to love.
A dance of souls, entwined in grace,
We find our home in this vast place.

Colors blend, horizons bend,
In the embrace that has no end.
With open arms, we face the dawn,
In every heartbeat, we're reborn.

Together we transcend the night,
Lost in wonder, lost in light.
The infinite whispers, soft and clear,
In the embrace, we hold what's dear.

Heartbeats in the Night

In shadows deep, we softly tread,
Whispers dance, the dreams are fed,
With every pulse, the world aligns,
Entwined in fate, where love defines.

The clock ticks slow, as if to tease,
Each fleeting moment brings us ease,
Stars overhead, a silent guide,
In this embrace, we shall confide.

The night is ours, a sacred space,
With stolen glances, time we trace,
Your heart's rhythm, a soothing balm,
Within this hush, we find our calm.

The moon's soft glow, a tender hue,
Reflects the love that blooms anew,
Each heartbeat sings, a sweet refrain,
In darkness wrapped, we break the chain.

Moonlit Recklessness

Under the moon's mischievous gaze,
We dance in shadows, lost in a haze,
With laughter that breaks the silent night,
Reckless souls, we take to flight.

Guided by stars, we run with glee,
Through fields of gold, wild and free,
Every heartbeat, a whispered dare,
In this moment, nothing can compare.

The night sings soft, our spirits rise,
As moonbeams twirl through starlit skies,
With fervor bright, we chase the dawn,
Bound by the thrill, we are reborn.

A fleeting sigh, a stolen kiss,
In chaos, we find our bliss,
With hearts ablaze, we forge ahead,
In moonlit recklessness, love is bred.

Secrets Beneath the Stars

Beneath the stars, we share our dreams,
In whispers soft, as night redeems,
The stories held, our souls' delight,
In shadows deep, secrets take flight.

With every glance, a truth unfolds,
In hidden corners, our fate molds,
The universe, a stage, so grand,
Together we carve, hand in hand.

Each twinkling light, a guiding star,
With hope and love, we've come this far,
As silence wraps, we dare to share,
The hidden paths, the love laid bare.

In every breath, a promise sewn,
Through whispered fears, we have grown,
Secrets bloom under night's embrace,
Together we find our sacred place.

Vows to the Wind

In twilight's glow, we make our vows,
To the gentle breeze that softly bows,
With laughter bright and eyes that shine,
We pledge our hearts, forever entwined.

The wind carries whispers of our fate,
A dance of lovers, never late,
In every gust, a promise flies,
To cherish, love, beneath the skies.

As stars above begin to gleam,
With hopeful hearts, we forge a dream,
In rustling leaves, our secrets blend,
With nature's breath, our love won't end.

Through changing seasons, strong and true,
We'll face the storms, me and you,
In every breeze, our souls will soar,
Vows to the wind, forevermore.

Boundless Dreams

In the stillness of the night,
Whispers of hope take flight,
Stars awaken in the sky,
Guiding hearts that dare to fly.

Fields of gold beneath the moon,
Crickets sing a soft tune,
A tapestry of wishes spun,
In the light of the setting sun.

Mountains rise, a path ahead,
With every step, we are led,
Embracing all that is unseen,
In the land of what could be.

Dreamers gather, hand in hand,
Making castles in the sand,
Paths that twist and turn with grace,
Reflecting dreams we all embrace.

In the end, it's love we find,
Uniting souls of every kind,
Boundless dreams, through night and day,
Eternal light will lead the way.

Echoes of Euphoria

Moments linger in the air,
A dance of joy, beyond compare,
Radiant laughter lights the way,
Chasing shadows far away.

Beating hearts in perfect time,
Life's sweet rhythm, pure and prime,
Every smile a spark divine,
In the echoes, we align.

Fragrant blooms in vibrant hues,
Nature whispers gentle cues,
Breezes carry soft refrains,
Washing over like warm rains.

Fires crackle, stories shared,
In each moment, love declared,
Journeys rich in every glance,
Holding hands, we weave a dance.

Together, we embrace the light,
In the dark, we shine so bright,
Echoes of euphoria sing,
In our hearts, we find the spring.

Dances in the Moonlight

Beneath the glow of silvery beams,
Together we weave our dreams,
Whispers carried on the breeze,
Dancing shadows among the trees.

Gentle laughter fills the night,
Magic swirls, a pure delight,
Every heartbeat, every turn,
In the fire of love, we burn.

Stars above our silent friends,
Guiding paths that never end,
With every step, the world fades,
In this moment, love cascades.

Feet entwined on grassy floors,
Nature's rhythm gently soars,
Bathed in silver, we are free,
In this dance, just you and me.

The moon smiles on our embrace,
In the night, we find our place,
Dances in the moonlight bright,
Forever etched in shared delight.

Threads of Yearning

Woven tales of heart and soul,
In the tapestry, we feel whole,
Each thread a story intertwined,
In every moment, love aligned.

Winds of change may twist and sway,
Yet hope remains, come what may,
Binding whispers in the night,
Threads of yearning take their flight.

Memories dance like fireflies,
Flickering, painting starry skies,
Chasing dreams across the land,
In threads of gold, together we stand.

Longing speaks in silent ways,
Carving paths through endless days,
With every heartbeat, every sigh,
Threads of yearning never die.

In the fabric of our fate,
Love's embrace will never wait,
Through the storms, we'll find our way,
Threads of yearning, here to stay.

Heartstrings and Kaleidoscopes

In the silence where dreams dance,
Colors swirl, caught in a glance.
Each heartbeat echoes a tune,
Weaving magic beneath the moon.

The laughter of children rings clear,
In this prism, there's nothing to fear.
Shadows play with light so free,
Binding our hearts, just you and me.

Moments captured, forever bright,
Painting the world in pure delight.
With every twist, love's embrace grows,
In the kaleidoscope, beauty flows.

Secrets whispered under the stars,
Binding our souls with silver bars.
Together we walk, hand in hand,
Creating a dreamland, so grand.

Heartstrings strum a gentle song,
In this universe where we belong.
With each glance, a new hope shines,
In our hearts, the world aligns.

Quest for the Unfathomable

In the depths where shadows hide,
The mind wanders, a curious guide.
Seeking truth in whispers of night,
Stars above, our dreams ignite.

Winding paths of ancient lore,
Each step reveals an open door.
With courage found in every stride,
The heartbeats echo, love our guide.

Mountains rise like giants tall,
In their presence, we stand small.
Yet within us lies a fire,
To explore the deep and aspire.

Mysterious waves call from afar,
Pulling us toward that shining star.
The oceans' depths and skies above,
In our journey, we find our love.

To seek the unknown, brave and bold,
Is the treasure more dear than gold.
In the quest for all that's vast,
We discover our futures, unsurpassed.

Love Letters to the Universe

In the stillness of the night,
I send my thoughts, taking flight.
Each star a message, soft and clear,
Whispering secrets for you to hear.

Galaxies spin with timeless grace,
In this vastness, we find our place.
Comets trail like dreams set free,
A love letter carried across the sea.

From mountains high to oceans deep,
The universe sings as we leap.
Every heartbeat, part of the rhyme,
In this harmony, we dance through time.

I write my wishes upon the skies,
In the moon's glow, my spirit flies.
Every twinkling star, a kiss,
In every moment, find our bliss.

With ink of stardust, paper of night,
I craft a world, warm and bright.
To the universe, my soul lays bare,
In love's embrace, we find our share.

Unbridled Aspirations

Across the valleys, dreams take flight,
Chasing the dawn, igniting the night.
With every breath, we dare to soar,
Our spirits longing, always more.

Mountains high and rivers wide,
In their presence, hope won't hide.
Each aspiration, a vibrant spark,
Guiding us through the endless dark.

Breaking chains that hold us fast,
Building futures, shadows cast.
In pursuit of all we aspire,
Together we build a world that inspires.

With open hearts and eyes so bright,
We transform fears into pure light.
The horizon calls with a whisper sweet,
In unity, we rise to our feet.

A tapestry woven with threads of gold,
Our dreams are brave, our spirits bold.
In every heartbeat lies our song,
Unbridled aspirations, where we belong.

Treasures of the Aspiring

In the heart where dreams reside,
Whispers of ambition glide.
Through the mist, they find their way,
Guiding souls to light of day.

A treasure map of stars above,
Each one shining, bright with love.
Hands reach high, the spirits soar,
Unlock the paths, and seek for more.

Chasing shadows, casting fears,
Embracing hopes, through all the years.
With every step, the light unfolds,
A story rich with dreams of gold.

Seek the gems in every trial,
Let your courage stretch a mile.
For in the depths of trials faced,
The treasures of the heart are placed.

Seeds of Unyielding Hope

In the soil where shadows dwell,
Planted dreams, we know so well.
Watered by the tears we shed,
From darkness sprout the seeds we spread.

Gentle winds will sing their tunes,
Guiding them 'neath sun and moons.
A tapestry of vibrant hues,
Each flower born from life's own dues.

The storms may rage, the nights may freeze,
Yet in our hearts, we find the ease.
Hope's anthem rises, ever bright,
A beacon through the endless night.

With every dawn, a chance to grow,
From tiny seeds, our spirits flow.
Unyielding strength in life's embrace,
Together we'll find our rightful place.

Reflections of the Undaunted

Mirrors hold the tales we weave,
Of battles fought, and moments grieved.
Yet in their depths, resilience shows,
A strength that in the heart still grows.

Each crack a mark of lessons learned,
In every scar, our fire burned.
The echoes of the brave remind,
That with each fall, we grow unconfined.

With courage clasped in steady hands,
We walk anew on shifting sands.
The past, a guide, not chains of fear,
Its whispered wisdom crystal clear.

Against the storms, we stand ablaze,
In unity, we find our ways.
Reflections bright of those undaunted,
In every clash, our spirits haunted.

Embers of Desire

In the quiet, embers glow,
A flicker of what we long to know.
Each spark ignites a distant fire,
Fueling up our heart's desire.

With every breath, the flames resound,
In whispers soft, our hopes are found.
They dance and sway, a rhythmic beat,
A symphony of dreams so sweet.

Fanned by winds of chance and fate,
The embers rise, they congregate.
Together bright, they brave the night,
In darkness, they become our light.

Through every storm that tries to quell,
The fire burns, we'll never dwell.
For in our souls, the embers sing,
A call to rise, and take to wing.

The Tapestry of Zeal

In threads of gold, we weave our dreams,
With passion's fire, it brightly gleams.
Each stitch a hope, each knot a fight,
Together we craft our own delight.

Through trials faced, our spirits rise,
With every tear, our strength defies.
We pull the colors from the night,
Creating patterns bold and bright.

With every heartbeat, the fabric grows,
In vibrant shades, our journey shows.
In unity, we stand so tall,
The tapestry sings; we hear its call.

In woven strands of love and grace,
We find our truth and rightful place.
The stories shared, a bond so real,
In every corner, we feel the zeal.

So let us weave with open hands,
A tapestry of diverse strands.
For in this art, we find our worth,
The tapestry of zeal, our rebirth.

Pathways of the Radiant

Beneath the stars, the pathways glow,
With silken light, where dreams can flow.
Each step we take, a chance to soar,
In radiant paths, we crave for more.

Through forests deep and valleys wide,
The whispers of hope become our guide.
With hearts ablaze, we seek the beam,
In every turn, we find the dream.

The dawn awakens with vibrant hues,
As golden rays chase off the blues.
Each journey's start, a sacred rite,
In pathways of the radiant light.

With every moment, we come alive,
In each connection, we begin to thrive.
With laughter shared and stories spun,
The pathways shine, for we are one.

So walk with courage, hearts held high,
In radiant paths, we'll learn to fly.
Through every shadow, every shade,
Our spirits dance; the light won't fade.

Thoughts on the Edge of Daydreams

On whispering winds, thoughts take flight,
As daydreams dance in soft twilight.
In quiet corners of the mind,
We seek the wonders yet to find.

With flickering stars, our hopes align,
Each thought a thread, a sign divine.
In fragments gathered, visions blend,
Where reality meets what might transcend.

In gentle waves of crystal skies,
The world transforms; the heart complies.
Each dream a spark, a flicker's glow,
On edges soft, new worlds we sow.

So let us linger on this line,
Between the real and the divine.
For in these moments, we expand,
Thoughts on the edge, by dreams we stand.

Awake but dreaming, lost in thought,
In daydreams found, a freedom sought.
With open hearts, we sail the streams,
Exploring life's enchanting themes.

The Canvas of Existence

Brushstrokes bold on life's broad page,
In vibrant hues, we craft our stage.
With every hue, a story told,
On canvas bright, dreams unfold.

In splashes wild, we laugh and cry,
Each stroke a moment, passing by.
With every mark, the soul takes flight,
In canvas realms, we find our light.

Colors blend, and shadows play,
In life's mosaic, come what may.
With daring hearts, we paint our role,
The canvas speaks; it holds our soul.

From gentle strokes to wild embrace,
Life's masterpiece reflects our grace.
With open hands, we seek and strive,
The canvas hums; we're truly alive.

So let us paint with strokes so free,
In every shade, our destiny.
The canvas of existence waits,
For each of us to shift the fates.

Mosaic of Memories

In the corners of my mind,
Colors blend and shift,
Moments etched in silence,
A canvas made of drift.

Laughter echoes softly,
Whispers of the past,
Every shard a story,
A shadow that will last.

Old photographs lie scattered,
Time's embrace holds tight,
Fragmented but together,
Each piece caught in light.

In this patchwork of feelings,
Love and loss entwined,
A heart that beats in rhythm,
With threads that fate designed.

Through these vivid colors,
I wander, lost, yet free,
Each brushstroke tells a tale,
Of who I came to be.

The Language of Dreams

In twilight's soft embrace,
Whispers silently flow,
Between the veils of slumber,
Where hidden visions grow.

Stars sing in the darkness,
A melody so light,
Guiding fragile visions,
Through the endless night.

Words unformed and fleeting,
Crafted in the air,
Painting realms for wanderers,
Suspended in a flair.

Echoes of the heartbeats,
In shadows dance and play,
Their stories weave together,
In colors bold and gray.

Awakening at dawn,
With dreams that softly gleam,
I hold the threads of night,
In the sunlight's warm beam.

Fragments of Forever

Beneath the stars we gather,
In the silence of the night,
Each glance a fleeting promise,
Each touch a spark of light.

Eternity feels fragile,
In moments lost in time,
Yet every breath, a heartbeat,
In rhythm and in rhyme.

Time folds like a paper,
Creases mark our way,
In every scar a story,
We carry through the day.

Collecting dreams like petals,
Each fragrance rich and rare,
A bouquet of our journeys,
Our moments laid bare.

Though seasons may be changing,
And sun may set or rise,
In fragments, love remains,
Reflected in our eyes.

The Taste of Wildness

In the rustle of the leaves,
A symphony begins,
With whispers of the wild,
Where untamed joy spins.

Underneath the wide, blue sky,
The spirit roams so free,
In the dance of wildflowers,
Nature's jubilee.

The taste of rain and earth,
A sweetness in the air,
With every breath a promise,
Of life beyond compare.

Mountains stand as guardians,
Of secrets deep and vast,
In the embrace of wildness,
I find my heart anchored fast.

With every step I wander,
Where rivers carve the land,
I savor wild adventures,
The taste of nature's hand.

The Peak of Adventure

Up high where the eagles soar,
The winds whisper tales of yore.
Each step a dance, each breath a thrill,
The heart races, the spirit's will.

Mountains rise, a challenge bold,
Stories of courage waiting to be told.
With every view, a dream ignites,
In the arms of nature, pure delights.

A path unknown, the map unwritten,
Into the wild, our souls are smitten.
The call of the wild, a siren's song,
On this journey, we all belong.

Stars above guide the night,
In the silence, we find our light.
From summit's edge, we feel alive,
Embrace the journey, the spirit thrives.

At the peak, we stand as one,
Bathed in the glow of the setting sun.
A toast to the heights, where we ascend,
In this adventure, let's never end.

Nurtured by Wonder

Beneath the boughs where shadows play,
Curiosity leads the way.
A world unfolds, vibrant and bright,
In the heart of nature, pure delight.

Whispers of magic in the air,
Every corner has tales to share.
The flowers dance, the streams hum sweet,
In this garden, life feels complete.

Eyes wide open, we chase the light,
In the stars above, we find our sight.
Each moment cherished, each heartbeat clear,
Nurtured by wonder, we lose our fear.

Children's laughter echoes around,
A symphony of joy, magical sound.
In the embrace of this sacred land,
With wonder's spark, together we stand.

Time flows gently, like a stream,
In every shadow, a hidden dream.
Together we wander, hearts intertwined,
Nurtured by wonder, our souls aligned.

The Flame of Ambition

In the depths where passions burn,
A flicker ignites, a fierce return.
Dreams sow seeds in fertile ground,
With every heartbeat, the fire's found.

Ambition's spark, a guiding light,
Through darkest paths, it shines so bright.
Fuel the desire, let it soar,
In the chase, we learn to explore.

Obstacles rise, but we stand tall,
The flame within will never fall.
With every setback, our spirits grow,
Through the ashes, our strength will glow.

Burning brightly, refusing to fade,
In the dance of life, our plans are laid.
With vision clear and courage strong,
The flame of ambition drives us along.

In unity, we find our way,
Chasing dreams, come what may.
Together we rise, and together we fight,
With the flame of ambition, we reach new heights.

Footprints on the Sand

Along the shore where waves embrace,
We leave our footprints, a fleeting trace.
The tide rushes in, then takes away,
Memories linger, though they sway.

With each step, stories unfold,
Of sunlit days and nights of gold.
Echoes of laughter, whispers of love,
As seagulls dance in skies above.

The sun dips low, painting the scene,
In hues of crimson, gold, and green.
Each grain of sand a moment passed,
In life's vast ocean, we are cast.

Waves of time, they come and go,
Yet footprints linger, a gentle glow.
In the embrace of the sea's caress,
We forge our path, we find our rest.

So let us walk hand in hand,
Together we'll traverse this land.
With every footprint, a bond we create,
In the sand of time, our love will sate.

The Symphony of Longing

In shadows deep where whispers dwell,
A melody of dreams will swell,
The heartbeats echo, soft yet strong,
In every note, we find our song.

The distance pulls, a gentle thread,
With every sigh, the silence spread,
We dance in time, two souls apart,
Yet bound together, heart to heart.

Through twilight's glow, our hopes ignite,
A symphony beneath the night,
Each longing glance, a spark of fire,
We chase the whispers of desire.

As stars align in cosmic grace,
We search for love in every place,
With every turn, our paths collide,
In the sweet harmony, we bide.

A tune of loss, a song of gain,
In longing's depths, we feel the pain,
Yet in the ache, we find our peace,
The symphony will never cease.

Tapestry of Emotions

Threads of gold in a vibrant weave,
Emotions dance, they twist and cleave,
In every tear, a story told,
In every joy, a spark, a gold.

The colors blend, they ebb and flow,
A spectrum wild, a vibrant show,
Through hues of happiness and strife,
We stitch together the quilt of life.

With every heartbeat, a new design,
In love and loss, our fates entwine,
The fabric strong, yet fragile too,
A tapestry made of me and you.

The threads may fray, but never break,
A binding force in every ache,
Through grays of doubt, the reds of fear,
We find our way, our hearts sincere.

In every stitch, a hope, a dream,
The fabric's fate is woven theme,
Together we create and mend,
A tapestry that has no end.

The Edge of Ecstasy

At dawn's first light, we stand and sway,
The world awakes, ready to play,
With every breath, the thrill ignites,
On the edge of dreams, we take flight.

In whispers soft, the ecstasy grows,
Through tangled paths, in spiraled throes,
With every touch, a spark divine,
In pleasures found, our hearts will shine.

Through wild abandon, we'll let go,
Embracing tides that ebb and flow,
The pulse of life, a roaring sea,
On edges sharp, we'll find the key.

With laughter bright, and eyes that gleam,
We chase the whispers of a dream,
In fleeting moments, time suspends,
Euphoria found, where love transcends.

At nightfall's kiss, together we'll stand,
Hand in hand, with hearts unplanned,
On the edge of a wild desire,
We dance as one, in endless fire.

Chasing the Horizon

The sun dips low, a fiery glow,
We chase the line where dreams will flow,
With every step, we cut the ties,
In every breath, the future lies.

As twilight paints the sky with gold,
In whispered winds, our tales unfold,
Each heartbeat draws us ever near,
The horizon calls, we have no fear.

Across vast fields where shadows roam,
We seek the paths that lead us home,
With open arms, and hearts so bold,
We chase the stories yet untold.

In twilight's grasp, we rise and fall,
With every echo, we heed the call,
A journey shared, a bond so strong,
In every note, we find our song.

With starlit skies, our dreams take flight,
Together we embrace the night,
In pursuit of what lies ahead,
We chase the horizon, hearts unthread.

Ephemeral Connections

Fleeting moments pass us by,
Laughter shared under the sky.
Whispers fade like morning dew,
Yet memories linger true.

Hands may touch, then slip away,
Bound by night, lost by day.
In a glance, a world can bloom,
Creating beauty from the gloom.

Like fireflies in summer's dance,
Glowing softly, lost in trance.
Each sparkle, a fleeting kiss,
Proof that love, though brief, exists.

In a crowd, we find our place,
Distance bridged in warm embrace.
Yet like dreams, they come and go,
Leaving echoes, soft and slow.

So hold these moments, let them stay,
In our hearts, they'll never fray.
Though ephemeral, they define,
The threads of life, a delicate line.

When Shadows Inspire

Beneath the moon, the shadows creep,
Secrets whispered, silence deep.
They dance along the ancient stone,
A world where fears and hopes are sown.

Painted darkness, sharp and bright,
A canvas wrought in pale moonlight.
Every shadow tells a tale,
Of whispered truths that never pale.

From silence springs a spark of art,
A haunting melody of the heart.
Embrace the night, let shadows guide,
Transforming what we often hide.

In twilight's grasp, the spirit roams,
In every shadow, a voice finds homes.
It teaches us to face our fight,
Finding courage amidst the night.

For in the dark, inspiration grows,
A pathway paved, where wonder flows.
So listen close, as shadows sing,
There's beauty in the fears we bring.

Mapping the Uncharted

With every step, a path unfolds,
A landscape painted in unknown holds.
Stars above, they light the way,
Guiding adventurers who dare to stray.

Across the peaks, through valleys deep,
Past rivers wide, where secrets sleep.
Curiosity, our constant friend,
In search of places with no end.

The map is drawn with whispers soft,
Each landmark shapes the dreams aloft.
Ink of night, the stories told,
Maps of heart, in visions bold.

With every journey, we unfold,
New stories carved from hope and gold.
A compass true, within our soul,
Guiding us to become whole.

In the uncharted, we find our place,
Embracing life at a steady pace.
For every step beyond the shore,
Is a glimpse of what life has in store.

The Language of the Wind

Whispers carried on the breeze,
Softly speaking through the trees.
A secret song, both wild and free,
The wind alone knows how to be.

It tells of journeys, far and wide,
Of soaring birds and changing tides.
Rustling leaves in gentle play,
A melody to guide the day.

In every gust, a story spins,
Of where it's been and where it grins.
It wraps around, a warm embrace,
And dances with time and space.

Listen close, to what it shares,
Echoes of dreams, unspoken prayers.
For in its breath, the world's designed,
A silent truth for hearts aligned.

So let the wind take you away,
To places where the heart can sway.
In its language, find your peace,
And let the chaos of life cease.

Horizons Beckoning Brightly

The dawn breaks with gentle light,
Colors dance, a stunning sight.
Birds take flight, the sky so wide,
Hope awakens, dreams collide.

Mountains call with peaks so high,
Waves crash down, a lullaby.
New roads stretch, untraveled lands,
Possibilities in our hands.

Every step, a chance to grow,
In the breeze, the wildflowers blow.
Time unfolds like petals fair,
Love and laughter fill the air.

Underneath this vast expanse,
Heartbeats quicken in the dance.
Together we will chase the sun,
Horizons shine, we will outrun.

Through the storms and through the night,
Hand in hand, our spirits bright.
Onward still, we chase the gleam,
Horizons beckon, spark the dream.

Chasing Shadows of the Heart

In twilight's grip, we start to roam,
Ghostly whispers, beckon home.
Flickering lights in darkened lanes,
Caught in echoes, love's refrains.

Footsteps fade on cobbled stone,
In shadows deep, we feel alone.
Yet in the stillness, secrets rise,
The heart knows where the truth lies.

Through alleys steep, and paths unknown,
Love's reflection brightly shown.
Like silver beams 'neath moonlit skies,
We chase the dreams that never die.

A gentle touch, a fleeting glance,
In shadows, we find our dance.
Together through the night's embrace,
We write our story, find our place.

In every sigh, the pulse, the art,
We chase the shadows of the heart.
For love will guide, through dark and light,
Together hands, we brave the night.

The Pulse of Experience

Time flows like a river's grace,
In moments lost, we find our place.
Every heartbeat tells a tale,
In life's adventure, we prevail.

Seasons shift, the world evolves,
In mysteries, our hearts resolve.
Colors fade, but memories last,
Lessons learned from shadows cast.

We paint our dreams across the skies,
With laughter's echo, love's replies.
Through trials faced and bridges burned,
The fire within us always turned.

Embrace the highs, endure the lows,
Through every wound, experience grows.
A tapestry of joy and strife,
The pulse of experience is life.

In every step, a rhythm's call,
Through valleys deep, we rise, we fall.
Together we shall weave the threads,
The pulse of experience, it spreads.

Embarking on Odyssey

With sails unfurled, we leave the shore,
The winds of change, they promise more.
Stars above our guiding light,
An odyssey through endless night.

Canvas sky, horizons wide,
In the unknown, we take our stride.
Tales of courage, whispers of fate,
Boundless journeys, never late.

Through stormy seas and tranquil waves,
In each adventure, the heart braves.
Treasures found, and lessons learned,
The fire of passion ever burned.

With every landmark, stories unfold,
In laughter shared, our spirits bold.
Together we plot our vibrant way,
Embarking on this grand array.

We chase the dreams beneath the sun,
In every glance, we find our fun.
An odyssey that never ends,
In every heart, a journey blends.

Embers of Devotion

In shadows soft, our whispers dwell,
Where love's warm glow begins to swell.
Through gentle nights and morning's light,
We find our way, hearts drawn so tight.

With every spark, a promise burns,
In quiet moments, the world turns.
Through trials faced and storms combined,
Our embers glow, forever entwined.

Each fleeting touch, a sacred vow,
In timeless space, we breathe and bow.
Our spirits dance, the fire grows bright,
In the tapestry of love's pure light.

No distance far can steal this flame,
For in our hearts, it knows no name.
With every heartbeat, we ignite,
The embers of our love's true might.

Whispers of the Heartbeat

In the hush of night, a voice calls near,
A promise woven, crystal clear.
With gentle beats, the echoes play,
They guide us through the veil of day.

Each pulse a note in the silent song,
Tells of the place where we belong.
Through every sigh, the world stands still,
A melody born of hope and will.

In shared breaths, our souls align,
Each whisper speaks a truth divine.
In rhythms soft, we find our way,
Through shadows deep to light's embrace.

With every thrum, our spirits soar,
Together we dream, forevermore.
Through every heartbeat, love is found,
In whispered tones, our joy knows no bound.

Chasing Wild Horizons

Beyond the peaks where eagles fly,
We chase the dreams that light the sky.
With every step, the world expands,
Adventure calls, we take a stand.

Through valleys deep, through rivers wide,
We find our strength, no fear to hide.
The sun ignites the dawn's embrace,
In wild horizons, we find our place.

With open hearts, we greet the day,
Embracing paths that lead the way.
In every heartbeat, whispers glow,
To chase the wild where wonders flow.

No road too long, no dream too far,
With stars above, we know who we are.
Together we run, unbound and free,
Chasing horizons, just you and me.

The Fire Within

In silence deep, a flame resides,
A light that whispers, never hides.
Through darkest nights and brightest days,
The fire within forever plays.

With every challenge, it roars to life,
A beacon strong amidst the strife.
Through pain and joy, it finds a way,
To light the path, to guide the stray.

Each flicker tells a tale of old,
Of dreams once lost and futures bold.
In quiet moments, hear it sing,
The fire within, our sacred spring.

With passion fierce, it paints the night,
In every shadow, it shines bright.
A force unyielding, we begin,
To fan the flames of the fire within.

The Pulse of Tomorrow

In whispers soft, the dawn awakes,
Where dreams converge, the future takes.
With every beat, a promise new,
The world unfolds in vibrant hue.

A path uncharted, stars aglow,
In shadows cast, the rivers flow.
Each moment flows, a tapestry,
Of hopes and fears, our destiny.

Hands join together, hearts ablaze,
In unity, we set the gaze.
Through trials faced, we rise and soar,
The pulse of life, forevermore.

In echoes deep, the ages blend,
A song of peace, our voices send.
The time ahead, our canvas wide,
With love and courage as our guide.

So take this heart, and dare to dream,
For tomorrow's light, a shining beam.
Together strong, we march as one,
To greet the dawn, the day begun.

A Symphony of Starlight

Underneath the velvet sky,
Where stars dance bright, and dreams can fly.
A symphony in silence plays,
Each note a wish, in cosmic rays.

With every twinkle, hopes arise,
Reflections of our deepest ties.
In harmony, the universe sings,
A gentle wind, the joy it brings.

As night unfolds, the stories share,
Of whispered love and visions rare.
In hidden realms, the wishes glow,
A chorus soft, the heart will know.

To wander lost in starry trails,
Where time stands still and magic sails.
In dreams we weave, a world anew,
A symphony of me and you.

So let the stars, our music guide,
With every pulse, our souls collide.
Immersed in light, the night ignites,
A symphony of starlit rites.

Breath of the Infinite

In every breath, the cosmos sighs,
A dance of life in endless skies.
The wind whispers secrets untold,
Of time and space, of dreams so bold.

From deepest depths to heights unknown,
The breath of life, a seed we've sown.
In silent moments, truth reveals,
A tapestry of what life feels.

In fleeting time, we find our place,
In every heartbeat, a gentle grace.
The universe cradles our fears,
And with each breath, we shed our tears.

So embrace the silence, let it flow,
In the breath of the infinite, we grow.
For in this moment, we are free,
As boundless as the deep blue sea.

In harmony with the stars above,
We find our paths, we learn to love.
With every breath, we rise, we soar,
In the infinite, forevermore.

Horizons of Hope

In distant lands where dreams take flight,
Horizons stretch with morning light.
Each step we take, a chance to see,
The beauty in our unity.

Through valleys deep and mountains high,
Our spirits soar, we reach the sky.
With every dawn, the promise shines,
Of brighter days, in endless lines.

Together we face the stormy seas,
With courage strong, we find our ease.
In heart and mind, we share the load,
On paths of light, the hope bestowed.

So let the winds of change now blow,
Through open hearts, our courage grows.
In every breath, we plant the seeds,
Of dreams fulfilled, of hope that leads.

To rise like sun upon the morn,
And greet the day, reborn, reborn.
With hands entwined, we'll shape our fate,
In horizons wide, we'll celebrate.

Fragments of Fervor

Whispers of dreams in the night,
Scattered like stars, lost from sight.
Passion ignites, a flame so bright,
Each spark dances, a fleeting delight.

Moments collide, hearts in a race,
Fragments of joy, we dare to embrace.
Captured in time, a fleeting grace,
Spirits entwined in a sacred space.

Tender are whispers, soft as a breeze,
Bound by the warmth of lingering ease.
Every heartbeat sings through the trees,
In pieces we find, love's gentle tease.

Journey of souls, we wander and roam,
Finding in fragments, a place called home.
Among the chaos, love's sweet poem,
Within each heartbeat, our hearts' true dome.

Echoes of fervor, never lose sight,
Each moment cherished, a pure delight.
Together we stand, through day and night,
Fragments of fervor, our souls take flight.

Flickering Flames of Desire

In the quiet dusk, a spark ignites,
A dance of shadows, the heart takes flight.
Flickering flames, soft whispers call,
Desires awaken, in love we fall.

Each gaze entwined, a story unfolds,
In the warmth of fire, our truth beholds.
Embers of longing, a heat so rare,
In moments of silence, love's sweet dare.

Under the stars, we share our dreams,
Flickering hopes, like radiant beams.
With every heartbeat, passion climbs,
In the rhythm of night, our souls chime.

Chasing the shadows, we're lost in time,
Flames of desire, a pulse sublime.
Through whispers and sighs, our spirits soar,
In the glow of the night, we crave for more.

Winds will carry our desires afar,
Yet in this moment, we are the stars.
Flickering flames, forever conspire,
To weave our hearts in entwined desire.

Symphony of the Chasing Spirit

Notes in the wind, a melody flows,
Chasing the light where the wildflower grows.
Laughter of nature, a vibrant refrain,
In the symphony's heart, we dance through pain.

As echoes resound, the spirit takes wing,
In the rhythm of life, our hearts boldly sing.
Chasing the dawn, where dreams come alive,
In the symphony's pulse, our spirits thrive.

Waves of emotion crash on the shore,
Harmonies linger, inviting us for more.
Each step we take, a note deeply played,
In the orchestra of life, together we wade.

From silence we rise, with courage anew,
A canvas of sound, a vibrant view.
Chasing our song, through shadows we glide,
In the symphony's arms, where our hearts reside.

Moments awaken, as spirits unite,
In every embrace, the future shines bright.
A symphony crafted, in freedom we soar,
Chasing the echoes, forever explore.

Sails Against the Wind

With sails unfurled, we chase the tide,
Against the wind, our spirits abide.
The horizon beckons, distant and blue,
In the heart of the storm, we find what is true.

Whispers of courage, carried so high,
Through tempest and treachery, we reach for the sky.
Each wave may challenge, each gust may bite,
Yet onward we sail, into the night.

Bound by our dreams, we weather the strife,
With hearts like anchors, we embrace this life.
Fighting for freedom, our journey's design,
In every heartbeat, the sea will align.

Stars guide our course, a celestial map,
Through shadows of doubt, we'll navigate gaps.
Sails against the wind, we forge our own way,
In every adventure, come what may.

With courage ignited, we rise and we bend,
In sails against wind, our spirits transcend.
Each moment we cherish, a story begins,
In the depths of the ocean, our journey spins.

Wings of the Heart

In twilight's glow, we find our grace,
With whispers soft, our dreams embrace.
The fluttering wings, they rise and soar,
A dance of love forevermore.

Through trails of stars, our spirits fly,
In every tear, a silent sigh.
With every heartbeat, hopes ignite,
We chase the dawn, we seek the light.

In joy and pain, we learn to feel,
Each moment shared, a sacred seal.
Together we weave a tapestry,
Of courage held, of hearts set free.

The sky above, a canvas wide,
Where every thought and dream can glide.
With wings of fire, we stand apart,
Two souls entwined, one beating heart.

In stillness found, we breathe anew,
In love's embrace, all skies turn blue.
With every flight, we touch the stars,
Wings of the heart, no distance far.

Beneath the Surface

In shadows deep, the secrets hide,
Where whispered thoughts and dreams collide.
The surface calm, a misleading peace,
Beneath the waves, the currents cease.

Ripples dance on the water's skin,
Where truths are shrouded, fears begin.
Beneath the gold, the dark will play,
Silent battles shadow the day.

With heavy hearts, we brave the dive,
To seek the treasures that keep us alive.
In depths unknown, our souls will find,
The echoes of the past intertwined.

Through murky shallows, our visions clear,
We face the tides, confront the fear.
With every breath, we rise and fall,
Beneath the surface, we heed the call.

So let us plunge and not retreat,
For every heartbeat makes us complete.
In the stillness, we'll learn to see,
The beauty found beneath the sea.

Savoring Life's Nectar

The morning sun brings golden light,
With every smile, the world feels right.
In simple joys, our hearts expand,
We sip the moments, hand in hand.

Like honey drips from nature's grace,
We find a rhythm, a sweet embrace.
With laughter shared, the hours blend,
In every sip, new dreams ascend.

The fragrance blooms in gardens near,
In each kind word, the heart will cheer.
We dance through seasons, rich and free,
Savoring life's sweet reverie.

With every taste, a memory made,
In fleeting seconds, love won't fade.
The spice of life, it stirs the soul,
As we collect the moments whole.

So let us feast on every thrill,
In simple pleasures, we find the fill.
With grateful hearts, we shall explore,
Savoring life's nectar, forevermore.

Cacophony of Longing

In crowded rooms, the silence screams,
A symphony of broken dreams.
With every glance, a story spun,
In shadows cast, our hearts undone.

The echo lingers, the heart will ache,
A dance of hopes that can't forsake.
With longing eyes, we search the past,
For fleeting moments that fade so fast.

Where whispers fill the empty space,
In every pause, we chase a trace.
With every heartbeat, we breathe despair,
A cacophony hangs in the air.

Yet in the noise, a spark ignites,
A flicker blooms in darkest nights.
The yearning calls us to explore,
In every ache, we long for more.

So let the music swell and rise,
In every tear hides a surprise.
With every longing, we shall find,
The beauty woven in the blind.

A Prelude to Freedom

In shackles worn, we dream of flight,
Whispers call through the tranquil night.
Steps of courage, hearts ignite,
A dawn awaits, our spirits' might.

Through the shadows, hope will gleam,
Voices rise, united dream.
Fingers grasp the threads of fate,
In this moment, we create.

Chains dissolve, the sky expands,
With every heartbeat, freedom stands.
Together we will brave the storm,
In the light, our souls transform.

Mountains high, the valleys low,
Across the fields where wild winds blow.
A prelude sung, the future bright,
We take our flight into the light.

From silence born, a song of grace,
We claim our rightful, sacred place.
Hand in hand, our spirits soar,
A prelude to what lies in store.

Skyward Soars the Dreamer

The stars will sing when night is still,
A dreamer's heart, a boundless thrill.
With wings of hope, we rise and glide,
Embracing worlds where wonders bide.

Through clouds of doubt, our visions clear,
We chase the light, we conquer fear.
Each heartbeat echoes paths unknown,
In every step, the dream is sown.

The sky unfolds, a canvas vast,
Moments grasped, the shadows cast.
With every breath, we break the mold,
In colors bright, our futures bold.

We dance with stars, the moon our guide,
In the cosmos, we find our pride.
The dreamer soars with open eyes,
A journey vast beneath the skies.

Through every trial, we'll not recoil,
In every heartbeat, dreams uncoil.
Skyward dreams will never cease,
In endless flight, we find our peace.

Capturing Fleeting Moments

A whisper soft, the breeze at play,
Moments dance, then slip away.
In tender sights, we find our grace,
A fleeting smile, a cherished face.

A glance exchanged, the heart can sing,
In tiny worlds, our memories cling.
With every heartbeat, time stands still,
In captured time, we feel the thrill.

Sunrise fades into the dusk,
Fragments live where love is husk.
A fleeting touch, a love once shared,
In echoing hearts, our dreams declared.

In the silence, memories weave,
Threads of time, they share and cleave.
A photograph, a stolen glance,
In every heartbeat, fleeting chance.

We hold the moments, dear and tight,
In laughter's glow, in shadows' light.
Time may flee, yet love remains,
In fleeting moments, joy sustains.

Explorations of the Heart

A journey deep, the heart will dare,
In every beat, a truth laid bare.
Through valleys low and mountains high,
We seek the echoes, the reasons why.

With open arms, we greet the night,
In whispers soft, the souls take flight.
Under the stars, we find our way,
In silent vows, our fears allay.

From every ache, a lesson born,
Through broken paths, our spirits worn.
Yet in the shadows, light will gleam,
In every tear, we find our dream.

Explorations vast, we dare to roam,
In every heartbeat, we find our home.
Love's gentle hand will guide us near,
In cradled whispers, we draw near.

The heart's vast map, its secrets hold,
Through every story, new and old.
An endless quest, our spirits dart,
Together united, explorations of the heart.

Whispers of the Heart

In twilight's hush, secrets softly weave,
A melody sweet, where shadows believe.
Gentle sighs linger, like echoes in air,
A language unspoken, beyond mere despair.

Through silence they dance, emotions unfold,
Stories of love that are timid yet bold.
In the chambers of longing, the whispers reside,
Guiding the heart, where true feelings abide.

With each breath a story, with each glance a spark,
Illuminating paths in the depths of the dark.
In a moment of stillness, the truth is revealed,
Whispers of the heart, our secrets concealed.

Hope swells like tides, in a tempest's embrace,
Promises linger, with time's gentle grace.
In the rhythm of silence, love's essence we'll find,
Whispers entwined, souls softly aligned.

So listen intently, let your spirit ignite,
For in whispered confessions, the heart takes flight.
In delicate murmurs, our destinies chart,
Embracing the whispers that dwell in the heart.

Dancing in the Firelight

Beneath the starlit sky, shadows sway,
Flames flicker and twist, as night turns to day.
Footsteps upon embers, the thrill of the night,
In the warmth of the moment, spirits take flight.

Laughter like music, echoes all around,
Holding on to dreams where lost souls are found.
With every turn, the flames rise high,
A dance with the night, beneath a velvet sky.

Hearts in rhythm, a pulsing desire,
Together we twirl, lost in the fire.
The glow of the embers, a magical light,
Guides us through darkness, igniting the night.

As shadows surrender, the dawn draws near,
Glimmers of hope chase away all the fear.
In the dance of the fire, we find our way home,
Together we wander, no more need to roam.

With each flicker fades, the night's sweet delight,
But memories dance on, in hearts ever bright.
So cherish the moments, let love's flame burn,
For in dancing together, our souls ever yearn.

Colors of the Soul

In a world painted vibrant, hues intertwine,
Emotions take form, like the sweetest of wine.
Blues whisper calm, red ignites the fire,
Colors of the soul, reflecting desire.

Yellows of laughter, warm as the sun,
Greens of the forest, where healing begun.
Each stroke tells a story, deep, rich, and bright,
Canvas of life, a remarkable sight.

Mysteries carried in a palette of dreams,
From the shadows emerge, the light softly gleams.
Together they mirror, in harmony's play,
The colors unite, chasing grayness away.

Violet whispers secrets, profound and wise,
Turquoise dances softly, like stars in the skies.
Every color a feeling, each shade a refrain,
In the spectrum of living, love conquers the pain.

So paint with abandon, let the heart be your guide,
In the gallery of life, let your spirit abide.
For the colors of the soul, vibrant and free,
Sing the song of existence, in harmony.

Unbridled Dreams

In the realm of the night, where hopes take flight,
Wings of ambition soar into the light.
Visions unfurl like the petals of spring,
Unbridled dreams beckon, our spirits to sing.

Through valleys of doubt, and mountains of fear,
The whispers of wanting beckon us near.
Chasing the shadows, we rise from the ground,
With hearts forged in courage, our freedom is found.

Every heartbeat a rhythm, every thought a spark,
Guiding the way through the vast, endless dark.
With eyes full of wonder, we paint the unseen,
In the tapestry woven from unbroken dreams.

So gather your courage, let the journey ignite,
For in the pursuit of our passions, we fight.
With laughter and tears, we embrace the theme,
This beautiful journey, our unbridled dream.

Together we'll wander, no limits in sight,
With hearts intertwined, we'll dance in the light.
In the tapestry bright, where hopes intertwine,
We'll dance through the canvas – your heart next to mine.

The Colors of Zeal

In the dawn's warm embrace, we rise,
With dreams painted bright, like the skies,
Every hue whispers tales of our fight,
A canvas of passion, glowing with light.

Fires of ambition ignite deep within,
Chasing the shadows, refusing to sin,
We dance to the rhythm of hearts that gleam,
In the tapestry woven, we color our dream.

Emerald greens of hope on the scene,
Rich burgundy reds, the courage we glean,
Through valleys of doubt, we travel the road,
With brushes of faith, we lighten the load.

Golden yellows burst forth with a grin,
Merging together, we're destined to win,
The spectrum of zeal, forever to shine,
In the gallery of life, our spirits align.

Serenade of the Soul

Beneath the stars, we gently sway,
Melodies soft, guiding our way,
With whispers of love that caress the night,
Awakening dreams, taking flight.

In the silence, our hearts intertwine,
A harmony pure, in rhythm divine,
Notes that linger, echoing soft,
In the symphony grand, we rise aloft.

Every heartbeat brings forth a song,
Carried by winds, where we belong,
With verses of hope, we weave our tale,
In the serenade sweet, we will not fail.

Through the shadows, our voices rise,
Stars serenade us, lighting the skies,
In the quiet hours, we find our goal,
A timeless embrace, the dance of the soul.

Unwritten Manifesto

On pages blank, our thoughts take flight,
Fleeting whispers, igniting the night,
Destinies waiting to be set free,
In the ink of our dreams, we choose to be.

Rejecting the past, we shape anew,
With every heartbeat, a vision in view,
A manifesto carved in the air,
A call to the brave, the willing to dare.

With courage, we pen the stories bold,
In colors of truth, in shades of gold,
A legacy etched in the hearts of those,
Who rise with conviction, as the world knows.

Unfolding the future, we gather as one,
A chorus of voices, brighter than sun,
In unity strong, we rise, we will fight,
For the unwritten pages, our guiding light.

Roaring for Tomorrow

With thunderous hearts, we stand united,
In echoes of hope, the fears ignited,
Voices raised loud, a fierce battle cry,
For freedom and justice, we will not die.

Through storms and shadows, our spirits ablaze,
Marching together, this newfound phase,
With strength in our laughter, forward we go,
Our dreams like lions, before us they grow.

The winds of change shift, urging the bold,
In the spirit of fire, no story untold,
With banners unfurled, we embrace the fate,
For a brighter tomorrow, we shall create.

In the echoes of history, we carve our way,
With hearts as our compass, a brighter day,
Roaring for freedom, our spirits soar high,
For tomorrow is waiting, beneath the vast sky.

Whirlwinds of Emotion

In shadows dance the fleeting sighs,
Passions rise beneath the skies,
A tempest brews within the soul,
Churning waves that take their toll.

Whispers echo, fierce and bright,
Caught in currents, lost in flight,
Grief and joy entwined as one,
A battle fought, but never won.

Eyes like storms, they flare and gleam,
Love can shatter, break the dream,
Yet from the chaos, blooms the light,
Every scar a tale of might.

Through every pulse, the heart will race,
In every heartbeat, find your place,
The whirlwind spins; we all must face,
A dance with fate, a sweet embrace.

So ride the waves, embrace the gale,
In every storm, let courage sail,
For in this whirlwind, truths reside,
And from the currents, hope will guide.

The Heart's Compass

In the silence, whispers call,
A guiding light to one and all,
With every choice, a path to trace,
The heart's true north, our sacred space.

Through valleys deep and mountains high,
The compass spins, but never lies,
Each breath a sign, each glance a clue,
For love will lead us, pure and true.

When shadows fall and doubts arise,
Trust in the pull, look to the skies,
The stars above ignite the way,
A map of dreams, a bright array.

With open hearts, we'll find our course,
A journey fueled by love's great force,
For in this quest, we're never lost,
Each step we take, no matter the cost.

So let the heart be your guiding star,
Through every trial, no matter how far,
For every beat shall set us free,
In love's embrace, our destiny.

Threads of Inspiration

In twilight's glow, ideas spark,
With woven dreams, ignite the dark,
Threads of wisdom intertwined,
In every heart, a story lined.

Colors dance upon the loom,
Inspiration blooms, dispelling gloom,
A tapestry of hopes and fears,
Stitched together through the years.

With every stitch, a vision grows,
A whisper caught where silence flows,
Hands create what minds conceive,
In every thread, we dare believe.

As patterns twist, new forms emerge,
A fusion born from love's great urge,
In every knot, the past aligns,
In threads of fate, our future shines.

So gather threads, embrace the art,
With each creation, heal the heart,
For in this fabric, life unfolds,
A tapestry of dreams retold.

Journey into the Unknown

With every step, the path reveals,
The thrill of life, the heart it steals,
Into the mist, where shadows play,
A daring chance, we leap and sway.

Uncharted waters call our name,
With hearts aflame, we stake our claim,
The horizon beckons, wild and free,
In the unknown, we learn to be.

Mountains rise, and valleys dip,
With every fall, we feel the grip,
Of fear and hope, they intertwine,
In every challenge, strength we find.

Though doubts may swirl like autumn leaves,
In courage's embrace, the spirit believes,
For every turn, a lesson waits,
In every fear, a chance creates.

So venture forth, embrace the wild,
For in the unknown, we're all but child,
With open hearts, let journeys start,
In every road, the map is art.

Rhythms of the Heart

In shadows deep, the heart does beat,
A silent song, a pulse so sweet.
With every thrum, a tale unfolds,
Of dreams and hopes, of love untold.

Through whispers soft, it finds its way,
In moments lost, in light of day.
Each rhythm sways, each note does play,
A dance of souls, in bright array.

A symphony of joy and pain,
In each refrain, we rise again.
The heart's true song, a guiding star,
In empty nights, it carries far.

With open arms, we heed the call,
The rhythm flows, we stand so tall.
In every beat, a chance to start,
In the cadence of the heart.

So dance along, embrace the sound,
Let love's sweet music wrap around.
In every heartbeat, life's embrace,
The rhythm of our shared grace.

Flames Beneath the Surface

Beneath the calm, the fire wakes,
A flicker born from hidden stakes.
Whispers of heat in shadows play,
While silence shrouds the chess we sway.

With every spark, a story ignites,
A dance of flames in fragile nights.
The warmth ascends, but danger brews,
In hearts of ice, the chill ensues.

Beneath this layer, passions churn,
A radiant flame, for which we yearn.
To stoke the fire, to feel the glow,
Is to invite the dance of woe.

Yet through the heat, a courage blooms,
In the furnace of our rooms.
To let the blaze consume our doubt,
And rise anew, with strength throughout.

So fan the flames, embrace the heat,
In every pulse, in every beat.
For within the furnace, life's embrace,
Is where we find our truest grace.

Journey Through Wildflowers

In fields of gold, where wildflowers sway,
A path unfolds, in bright array.
Each blossom sings, a vibrant song,
A journey starts, where hearts belong.

With gentle breeze, the petals dance,
In sunlit dreams, we find our chance.
To wander far, where nature reigns,
And draw from earth, the joys it gains.

The colors blend, a painter's dream,
In every hue, a life redeemed.
As blossoms bloom, we shed our fears,
In fragrant air, we find our tears.

Through winding paths and whispered tales,
We traverse realms as love prevails.
In petals soft, our secrets shared,
In nature's arms, we are prepared.

With every step, new wonders grow,
In wildflower fields, we learn to flow.
So journey on, let spirits rise,
In nature's dance, our hearts will fly.

The Art of Daring

To dare is to leap, to take a chance,
To dance with fate, to join the dance.
In boldest strokes, we paint our dreams,
With every breath, the spirit gleams.

Through valleys deep, on mountains high,
We face the clouds, we touch the sky.
In trembling hands, we craft our fate,
With courage found, it can't be late.

With every risk, we gather grace,
In daring steps, we find our place.
To live out loud, to break the mold,
Is to embrace the brave and bold.

The whispers doubt, yet still we rise,
In every fall, we claim the prize.
For in each bruise, a lesson gleams,
In art of daring, we shape our dreams.

So let us soar, let barriers fade,
In daring hearts, foundations laid.
For life's a canvas, paint it bright,
In every heartbeat, claim your light.

The Light Between Shadows

In twilight's embrace, we find our way,
Soft whispers of hope, where dreams sway.
Shadows cast long, yet we hold tight,
Guided by the glow of fading light.

A flicker ignites in the heart's core,
Illuminating paths we can explore.
In every pause, a chance to grow,
Revealing secrets the dark won't sow.

Hands reach for warmth amid the chill,
Every heartbeat speaks of will.
With courage, we face the unseen dread,
Drawing strength from what lies ahead.

Through clouds of doubts, we navigate,
Embracing the fears that tempt our fate.
Each moment breathes, alive and true,
In the light between shadows, hope renews.

So let us dance where the light meets night,
Finding solace in finesse and flight.
With every step, the world unfolds,
In the warm embrace of stories told.

A Spark in the Darkness

In the night's silence, a whisper ignites,
A lone spark flickers, defying the blights.
From embers of hope, a flame starts to rise,
Illuminating dreams beneath starlit skies.

Every shadow casts a tale of despair,
Yet the spark dances, seeking to share.
It leaps and it twirls, with grace unconfined,
Chasing away darkness, leaving fears behind.

In the heart's valley, quiet and deep,
The spark burns brightly, rousing our sleep.
It whispers of courage, it sings of the fight,
Guiding the lost with its steadfast light.

When faced with the storm, we clutch to that flame,
With passion and purpose, we rise without shame.
For each tiny flicker can blaze into fire,
Transforming the night into something higher.

Together we stand, with sparks in our hands,
Igniting the world, as destiny commands.
In the shadows, we forsake the doubt,
As the spark in the darkness lifts us out.

Vivid Echoes of Desire

In the chambers of longing, whispers reside,
Vivid echoes of dreams, where passions collide.
Every heartbeat resonates, a rhythm so true,
Tracing the outlines of me and of you.

Colors entwined, like a painter's best brush,
Painting the canvas where feelings rush.
With each gentle sigh, the palette expands,
Crafting a voyage through uncharted lands.

In the hush of the night, desires take flight,
Illuminating the darkness, a shimmering light.
With fervor we dance, with hearts intertwined,
Unraveling moments, sweet tales redefined.

The vividness swells in the silence we hold,
Every glance exchanged speaks more than words told.
In the depths of our souls, connections inspire,
Filling the voids with echoes of fire.

So let us embrace what the night has conspired,
And savor the echoes of passion, untired.
For in every heartbeat, a story will play,
In vivid echoes, we find our way.

The Dance of Possibility

In the garden of dreams, where wishes take flight,
The dance of possibility ignites the night.
With each tender step, the world starts to sway,
Unfolding a pathway, come what may.

In the laughter of breezes, we twirl and we spin,
Chasing the sun, where our journeys begin.
With hope as our lead, we glide through the air,
Embracing each chance, shedding every care.

Every heartbeat whispers, "Take the next chance,"
In the rhythm of life, we invite the romance.
With dreams like stars, we reach for the sky,
Creating our futures as we dance and fly.

In the tapestry woven, our stories converge,
The dance of possibility starts to emerge.
With fearless hearts, we break every chain,
Transforming the doubts into glorious gain.

So let the music play as we lose track of time,
In the dance of our lives, to each beat, we rhyme.
With laughter and love, let our spirits ascend,
In the embrace of the night, possibilities blend.

Flavors of Adventure

Winds from the mountains call my name,
A taste of the wild, sparkling and untamed.
Rivers of gold beneath the sun,
Every sip of life feels like a run.

Paths of the forest, shadows play,
Whispers of nature lead the way.
Cada turn brings a savory bite,
In each fleeting moment, pure delight.

Savory stories wrapped in dusk,
Fragrance of spices, a vibrant husk.
Every adventure, a feast of the soul,
A palette of dreams, make us whole.

Journey on trails, colors ignite,
Eyes wide open, captivating sights.
From mountains high to valleys low,
Flavors of adventure, forever flow.

With each new step, curiosity's song,
In the dance of life, we all belong.
Taste the joy, savor the thrill,
In every moment, the heart can fill.

Serenade of the Senses

Moonlit nights bring a soothing breeze,
Whispers of petals hugging the trees.
The fragrance of jasmine, sweet and light,
Kisses of colors in fading twilight.

Tastes of summer's ripe, juicy fruit,
Melodies echo through air, resolute.
Sounds of the ocean, waves dance and sway,
Every moment alive, a grand ballet.

Warmth of the sun kissing the skin,
A scintillating symphony begins.
The touch of the earth under bare feet,
In this serenade, life is sweet.

Watch as the stars twinkle and gleam,
Every sparkle ignites a dream.
Voices of nature, softly sing,
In this gentle chaos, joy takes wing.

Feel every heartbeat, a tender rhythm,
Guiding our souls, in perfect prism.
Through senses entwined, love finds its way,
In the serenade where dreams stay.

Echoes of the Heartbeat

In silence, a heartbeat softly calls,
Ripples of longing within the walls.
Memories linger like shadows at dusk,
Each pulse, a promise, each sigh, a husk.

Love's gentle tether pulls us near,
Filling the voids, quieting fear.
In every echo, a story unfolds,
Whispering truths that time beholds.

Through valleys hollow and mountains high,
The rhythm of life sings a lullaby.
Moments of laughter, tears intertwined,
In echoes of heartbeat, we are defined.

Navigate joy, navigate pain,
A dance through the storm, a walk through the rain.
In the crescendos, our spirits soar,
Every heartbeat is love, forevermore.

As shadows recede and dawn breaks bright,
Hold close the echoes, let them ignite.
For every heartbeat carries the spark,
An eternal promise, a light in the dark.

The Canvas of Yearning

Brush of the sunset paints the sky,
Strokes of desire, dreams floating high.
Canvas of longing, colors that blend,
Every heartbeat a message to send.

From whispers of hope to shadows of doubt,
Life's intricate art is what it's about.
A symphony of wishes in every hue,
Crafting the dreams we long to pursue.

In every tear, a spark of creation,
Colors collide in a wild sensation.
Each moment captured, a story anew,
On the canvas of yearning, we break through.

With bold strokes of courage, we face our fears,
Layering joy over shadows and tears.
In the gallery of life, we find our part,
Each vibrant canvas, a piece of the heart.

So let every wish be a brush in hand,
Paint your own world, let your heart expand.
On the canvas of yearning, bright and free,
Create your masterpiece, let it be.

Canvas of Colors

Brush strokes of red, blue and gold,
Dance on the canvas, stories unfold.
Nature's palette, vibrant and bright,
Each hue a whisper, living in light.

With every splash, a tale begins,
Of quiet joys, and gentle sins.
Swirling skies and fields of green,
Colors collide, a wondrous scene.

In golden dawn, each shade aligns,
A fleeting moment, where beauty shines.
Twilight beckons, hues start to blend,
A dance of colors, without an end.

With every stroke, emotions swell,
In this canvas, we're all compelled.
Artistry breathes, a life so pure,
A world transformed, forever sure.

Embrace the chaos, let it ignite,
In every corner, a love for the sight.
This canvas of colors, rich and free,
Reflects the essence of you and me.

Tides of Fire

Crimson waves crash on the shore,
Heat of passion, forevermore.
Dance of embers in the night,
Whispers of dreams take flight.

Flames flicker, casting shadows deep,
Secrets of hearts that we keep.
In the glow, true souls ignite,
A burning touch, a shared delight.

As the tides recede in time,
We find our strength, we start to climb.
Rising up from ashen sleep,
With every heartbeat, love runs deep.

From the fire, a phoenix flies,
Beneath the stars, we rise, we rise.
Embrace the heat, don't hesitate,
Together in flames, we soon create.

In the dusk, the fire will sway,
Tides of fire, guide our way.
Together we'll dance, hand in hand,
In this passionate, burning land.

Radiance of the Unseen

In silence dwells a radiant glow,
Hidden treasures, beneath the flow.
Soft whispers in the starlit night,
Unseen wonders, pure delight.

A heart that beats with gentle grace,
Mirrors the light in every space.
In shadows cast, true beauty lies,
In every tear, in whispered sighs.

Through clouds that veil the morning sun,
Resilience blooms, the fight begun.
Each moment holds a spark divine,
Shining brightly, through the brine.

The unseen threads that weave our fate,
Entwine our souls, a bond so great.
Within the depths, we find our way,
Through radiant paths, come what may.

In the quiet, listen close,
To the tales that life can boast.
For in the shadows, love is gleaned,
In the radiance of the unseen.

The Fireflies' Whisper

In twilight's hush, the fireflies glow,
A dance of lights, an evening show.
Soft flickers weave through the trees,
Carrying secrets upon the breeze.

Whispers of magic in the air,
Stories shared without a care.
Each little spark, a gentle sigh,
Illuminating dreams as they fly.

In the stillness, hearts take flight,
Guided by the stars in their light.
The night unfolds, a canvas wide,
While fireflies twinkle, joy and pride.

A chorus of laughter fills the night,
With every flicker, a pure delight.
In this moment, all feels right,
In the dance of fireflies, hearts unite.

As morning draws, their glow must fade,
Yet in our hearts, their light is laid.
The fireflies' whispers ever near,
Echoes of joy we'll always hear.

Love Letters to the Universe

In the silence, my whispers soar,
To the stars, I write, forevermore.
Each heartbeat dances with cosmic grace,
In this vast, endless space.

I pen my dreams in the midnight sky,
With every spark, I dare to fly.
Laughter echoes through the void,
In love, the universe is joyed.

Galaxies swirl, stories untold,
With every letter, my heart unfolds.
Wishes woven in starlit thread,
To the cosmos, my hopes are fed.

Oh, universe, hear my plea,
In this dance of infinity.
Your light guides me through the night,
In love, I find my eternal flight.

Together we swirl, a radiant blend,
In the expanse where souls transcend.
With love letters, I paint the skies,
In silence, our connection lies.

Unfurling the Spirit

In twilight's glow, the spirit wakes,
With every breath, the silence breaks.
Petals of hope begin to bloom,
As hearts ignite within the gloom.

A whisper stirs the ancient trees,
Calling forth the gentle breeze.
As shadows dance, a light appears,
Guiding us through hidden fears.

In the stillness, wisdom flows,
Like rivers where the wild wind blows.
Threads of life begin to weave,
In the depths, we learn to believe.

Awakening dawn, embrace the day,
Let colors spread in joyful sway.
Unfurling dreams, let voices rise,
In every soul, a sacred prize.

We rise as one, a symphony,
Through the valleys, wild and free.
With open hearts, we claim our fate,
Unfurling spirits, we celebrate.

The Quest for Meaning

In the stillness, questions stir,
Why we wander, yet never blur?
Chasing shadows of the past,
Searching for truths that long will last.

Through winding roads and tangled trees,
We seek the whispers in the breeze.
Each moment holds a hidden key,
Unlocks the door to destiny.

Echoes of laughter, traces of tears,
Carving paths through the doubts and fears.
With every heartbeat, we draw near,
In restless minds, we persevere.

The stars above, they flicker bright,
Guiding souls through the darkest night.
In the tapestry of time, we find,
Threads of purpose, love intertwined.

Together we search, hand in hand,
Every question, a grain of sand.
In the quest for meaning, we unite,
As seekers of truth, we ignite.

Burning Bright

In the heart of night, a spark ignites,
Fueling dreams with radiant lights.
Every flicker, a tale unfolds,
Of passion, courage, and love untold.

Through trials faced and shadows cast,
Our spirits rise, we hold fast.
The fire within, a sacred guide,
In every heartbeat, it resides.

Let the flames dance, let them soar,
Embrace the warmth, forevermore.
In unity, we find our might,
Together we shine, burning bright.

With every challenge, embers grow,
In the face of darkness, we glow.
A beacon of hope, we light the way,
In fierce resolve, we greet the day.

As stars align, our spirits blend,
With love's embrace, the journey transcends.
In the fires of life, our passions ignite,
Forever we burn, endlessly bright.

The Promise of Dawn

In the hush before the light,
A whisper breaks the night,
Colors paint the waking sky,
A new day draws us nigh.

Birds sing their early song,
To the world, they belong,
Hope rises with the sun,
A tale of dreams begun.

Morning dew on blades of grass,
Moments come and moments pass,
Shadows dance in golden streams,
World awakes from night's sweet dreams.

Each ray a gentle touch,
Reminds us we are much,
In the light, our fears dissolve,
Life's mysteries evolve.

With every dawn, renew our quest,
To seek the very best,
With open hearts we stand tall,
The promise beckons us all.

Flames of the Unsung

In shadows cast, they fight alone,
Silent voices, strength unknown,
Against the odds, they find their way,
In the dark, they seize the day.

With fire in their weary soul,
They rise, they struggle, they become whole,
Each scar a story, wisdom learned,
In the quiet strife, their passion burned.

Unsung heroes, tales untold,
In their hearts, a fire bold,
Against the tide, they push through pain,
In every loss, new hopes remain.

Flickering flames of courage rise,
In their eyes, the stars comprise,
Through the silence, they ignite,
A beacon in the darkest night.

Though the world may overlook,
Their spirit lives in every nook,
For in the quiet, power stirs,
Flames of the unsung, forever blurs.

The Exhibition of Existence

In the gallery of dreams and fears,
Each stroke holds the weight of years,
Moments freeze, like whispers caught,
Life's canvas, beautifully wrought.

Colors clash, yet harmony sings,
Life unfolds in curious flings,
Echoes linger in every frame,
An exhibition without a name.

Through laughter lines and sorrow's hue,
Each tale speaks of me and you,
Brushes dance with gentle grace,
We leave behind a trace of space.

In this vast, diverse display,
Each soul's journey finds its way,
The art of living, raw and true,
In every heart, a different view.

And as we walk from piece to piece,
We find the threads that bring us peace,
In the gallery of what we've known,
Together, we are never alone.

Open Skies of Hope

Beneath the vast, cerulean dome,
Hearts take flight, the world our home,
With every breath, the spirit soars,
In open skies, our essence pours.

Clouds drift softly, dreams in tow,
In gentle whispers, breezes blow,
As starlit paths begin to show,
Answers linger, hopes will grow.

Freedom dances on the breeze,
A symphony among the trees,
With open arms, we greet the sun,
In this embrace, we are all one.

Horizons beckon, call us near,
With open skies, we know no fear,
Each step we take, a chance to find,
The beauty woven, heart and mind.

So let us wander, wild and free,
Beneath the skies of destiny,
With every heartbeat, dreams ignite,
In open skies, our hopes take flight.

Heartbeats Against the Tide

In whispers soft, the echoes play,
Where dreams collide with night and day.
Together we will face the roar,
Each heartbeat sings, forevermore.

With every wave that crashes near,
We dance through doubt, we shed the fear.
The tide may rise, but so do we,
A symphony of wild and free.

The moonlight glimmers, guiding us on,
Through shadows cast until the dawn.
With passion fierce and spirits high,
We'll chase the stars across the sky.

A tapestry of all we've known,
Stitched with threads of dreams we've sown.
Each heartbeat marks a brand new stride,
Against the waves, we will abide.

In unity, our spirits blend,
As rhythms play, we shall ascend.
No storm can shake what we have found,
Our heartbeats strong, our souls unbound.

Dreamcatchers and Bright Tomorrows

In the quiet of the night, we weave,
Threads of hope, we dare believe.
Dreamcatchers hung with love and light,
To catch the whispers of our fight.

Through tangled paths and winding ways,
We find our strength in softer days.
With every dawn, new chances bloom,
A garden grown from fears that loom.

Stars above, they chart our course,
Guiding hearts with steady force.
In unison, our dreams take flight,
Together, chasing endless light.

With courage found in tender sighs,
We learn to rise where shadows lie.
Bright tomorrows wait in view,
A canvas fresh with every hue.

So we will dream with open hearts,
Embrace the magic as it starts.
With every breath, we claim our song,
In unity, where we belong.

Revelations in Motion

Through rippling waters, secrets glide,
Unfolding truths we cannot hide.
In every step, we find our place,
Revelations bloom, a soft embrace.

With every turn, the world reveals,
The hidden paths that time conceals.
In gentle whispers, lessons flow,
Awakening hearts, a steady glow.

In motion's grace, we learn to fly,
As branches stretch against the sky.
Through every struggle, joy resides,
In revelations, love abides.

So let the journey be our guide,
With open arms, we'll take the ride.
In moments shared, our spirits dance,
Revelations spark the soul's romance.

Together, we will brave the storm,
With hearts aligned, we'll keep us warm.
In every breath, the truth ignites,
Revelations in our sights.

Living in the Moment's Breath

In the pulse of now, we find our way,
Moments fleeting, come what may.
Each heartbeat sings a vibrant tune,
Living fully 'neath the moon.

With open eyes, we see the grace,
In every smile, in every face.
The present wraps like golden thread,
A tapestry of words unsaid.

With laughter bright, we chase the sun,
In simple joys that life has spun.
A fleeting touch, a shared embrace,
In every heartbeat, time we trace.

So take a breath, let worries fade,
In every moment, love is made.
The world awaits with arms unfurled,
Living now, we change the world.

With open hearts, we walk the line,
Each moment rich, forever shine.
In every breath, a gift we keep,
Living boldly, dreams run deep.